Railways & Recollections
The Midland Main Line in London,
Exploring from Hendon to St Pancras before electrification

Will Adams

CW00522274

© Will Adams 2022

First published in 2022

British Library Cataloguing in Publication Data

A catalogue record for this book is available from the British Library.

ISBN 978 1 85794 594 2

Silver Link Books
Mortons Media Group Limited
Media Centre
Morton Way
Horncastle
LN9 6JR
Tel/Fax: 01507 529535

email: sohara@mortons.co.uk
Website: www.mortonsbooks.co.uk

Printed and bound in the Czech Republic

Title page: **WEST HAMPSTEAD** signal box is seen on 19 September 1974.

Contents

Bibliography

I consulted many books from my own collection, and many websites, the most useful being listed below. Since this book was written during the Covid-19 'lockdown' in early 2021, location visits were impossible, so Google Earth proved invaluable as an indication of the present-day state of the Midland line.

Books
Bradley, Simon *St Pancras Station* (Profile Books, 2007)
Butt, R. V. J. *The Directory of Railway Stations* (Patrick Stephens Limited, 1995)
Hornby, Frank *London Suburban* (Silver Link Publishing, 1995)
Jackson, Alan A. *London's Termini* (David & Charles, 1969)
Lansley, Alastair et al, *The Transformation of St Pancras Station* (Laurence King Publishing Ltd, 2008)
Midland Railway Distance Maps, Volume 3 (Peter Kay, ND)
Rounthwaite, T. E. et al, *The Midland Railway London Extension 1868-1968* (Midland Railway London Extension Centenary Celebration Association, 1968)
Swift, John *British Railways Layout Plans of the 1950s, Volume 2* (Signalling Record Society, ND)
Tindall, Gillian *The Fields Beneath* (Maurice Temple Smith Ltd, 1977)
Weinreb, Ben and Hibbert, Christopher (eds) *The London Encyclopaedia* (Macmillan, 1983)
Williams, Frederick S. *Midland Railway: Its Rise and Progress* (1876, reprinted 1968, David & Charles)

Websites
British History Online: www.british-history.ac.uk
Disused Stations: disused-stations.org.uk
History of St Pancras International: stpancras.com

Introduction

The Midland Railway's extension to London from Bedford to St Pancras opened fully on 1 October 1868 (local trains had run via St Pancras Tunnel to Moorgate from 13 July). From then on, improvements and widenings were undertaken through to 1905. Sufficient land had been purchased at the outset for four tracks, and from opening there were four from St Pancras almost to Hendon, except through Belsize Tunnel. Two additional tracks were provided between St Pancras passenger and goods stations in 1870.

The intermediate stations opened in the London area on 13 July 1868 were Hendon, Finchley Road, Haverstock Hill, Kentish Town and Camden Road. On 2 May 1870 Child's Hill & Cricklewood (just Cricklewood from 1903) was added, together with Welsh Harp. West Hampstead (under various early names) followed on 1 March 1871. In 1884 Belsize New Tunnel was opened, and widening to six tracks was undertaken between St Paul's Road Junction and Carlton Road Junction, together with the addition of Tottenham North Curve towards Barking from the latter place. This was joined by the South Curve via Engine Shed Junction in 1900, to form a triangular junction. (There was also the Tottenham South Curve 'flyover' line from Kentish Town to Highgate Road and onwards to Barking, opened in 1870.) Further widening between Hendon and West Hampstead was completed by 1905. And thus, with all the associated sidings, yards and loco sheds, the Midland Main Line in London reached its greatest extent.

*

In the autumn of 1974 my wife-to-be and I rented our first flat, in Iverson Road, Brondesbury, just off Kilburn High Road in north-west London. For a railway enthusiast, it had a lot to recommend it: the North London Line at Brondesbury station ran past the bottom of the back garden, while Iverson Road was spanned by a large viaduct carrying the Bakerloo and Metropolitan Underground lines and the former Great Central line into Marylebone. At the top of Iverson Road, at West End Lane, was West Hampstead station on the Midland Main Line.

Being a West Midlands native, I knew little of the Midland line, but soon got to know it well. Although there was then still plenty of mechanical signalling to be found around the country, it was unusual to find a four/six-track main line still principally controlled by semaphore signalling. This clearly provided considerable operational interest, as well as being visually attractive.

I lost no time in spending spare hours exploring and photographing as much as I could of what remained to be seen. I spent many evenings watching the Midland and North London lines, as well as the Metropolitan/Bakerloo and Marylebone lines, from the grandstand of the public footpath crossing the Midland at Finchley Road. I was a keen 'poker-about' of old railway premises, and many ghosts of the recently passed Steam Age survived between Cricklewood and St Pancras.

St Pancras was one of the last London termini to receive modern signalling. In 1974 there were still signal boxes at Silk Stream Junction, Brent Junction Nos 1 and 2, Cricklewood, Watling Street Junction, West Hampstead, Finchley Road, Carlton Road Junction, Mortimer Street Junction, Engine Shed Junction, St Paul's Road Goods, Dock Junction and North London Incline. The route had become rather neglected, and still had that wonderful sooty, rather gloomy ambience of a steam-era main line.

Unfortunately I had a limited income and only

a Kodak Instamatic camera using colour slide cartridges, so the photographic results depended very much on the weather and the availability of good light. Thus some of the results were very disappointing, but the best (and the better among the mediocre) have been selected for use in this book, which has been an enjoyable and nostalgic revisiting of locations I first explored nearly half a century ago!

The photographs are supplemented by a selection of maps and plans. Some I purchased from the late-lamented Collectors Corner, a treasure trove of ephemera and larger items (even locomotive nameplates) housed in a gloomy warehouse at Euston station. Here also I bought a couple of redundant signal box diagrams after the boxes had closed in 1977/78 as a prelude to modernisation and electrification. One day I discovered in Swiss Cottage Public Library a bound large-scale 1951 BR map of the line from north of Cricklewood to St Pancras, giving a wealth of detail from every signal post and platelayer's hut upwards. I painstakingly copied this out and drew my own version on card, which ended up more than 20 feet long. A couple of extracts are included here.

Looking at that map it is astonishing to see the complexity of the railway layout between Silk Stream Junction, where the two pairs of tracks became three, and the buffer stops at St Pancras. Yards, sidings, loco sheds and intensive criss-crossing junctions were provided to cope with, to us, an unimaginable amount of freight traffic, especially coal, the capital's life-blood. The enormous cost and effort involved in providing the sometimes massive earthworks and brick-lined cuttings was all deemed worth it to maximise traffic, hopefully to the detriment of competitors. The aspirations and confidence of the railwaymen of that age are embodied in every brick, not least at St Pancras itself with its awe-inspiring trainshed and magnificent station buildings and hotel, haughtily looking down upon its relatively plain-Jane neighbour at King's Cross.

The old railway was people-sized and people-operated, and there is no denying that I miss the signal boxes and signals, the junctions and the grubby, neglected stations, and find the modern electric railway rather un-human and soulless. And while the modern railway undoubtedly provides a standard of service far better than what was on offer 50 years ago, I am so grateful to have been able to witness and photograph the twilight of a steam-age main line before it was transformed beyond recognition. I hope you enjoy this nostalgic exploration as much as I have enjoyed reliving, researching and writing about it.

NORTH OF MILL HILL Pre-electrification prelude: this picture is believed to have been taken from Selvage Lane, Apex Corner, looking south towards Mill Hill Broadway station some time in the early 1970s; the motorway had been extended south to Scratchwood in 1967. The cars of the era seem almost dwarfed by the motorway lanes, while a DMU heads south towards St Pancras on the Up Fast line. *BR(LMR)*

SILKSTREAM JUNCTION Our journey starts just short of 8 miles from the buffer stops at St Pancras. In the 1970s the four tracks of the Midland Main Line were still unbroken from Glendon South Junction, north of Kettering, to Silkstream Junction, where a pair of Goods lines were added. These additional two tracks needed to be on the down side of the formation, since the major goods facilities, including the St Pancras and Somers Town goods depots, and the junction at Cricklewood with the Midland & South Western Junction line to Willesden, Acton, and thence all points west and south (an important coal artery), were all on the down side. (The 'old' M&SWJ line is not to be confused with the railway of the same name linking Cheltenham and Andover.) As can be seen from this signal box diagram, this was cleverly arranged so that the new Goods lines left the Slow lines and 'flew' over the Down Local and Up and Down Fast lines, thus avoiding any conflicting movements on the level. The erstwhile Slow lines became the Local lines from here southwards. Note that Silkstream Junction didn't signal the Fast lines. By the late 1970s the box was hard against the extension of the M1 motorway, so difficult to photograph except from a passing train. The signal box closed on 11 June 1978. *Author's collection*

HENDON This BR track plan dated 1968 shows the new Goods lines dropping down to join the main formation just north of Hendon station. As can be seen, a fan of sidings ('Hendon New Sidings' – the 'Old Sidings' were on the opposite, east, side of the main line) once filled the area between. In more recent years a long chord has replaced the sidings area, linking the Up Goods to the Down Fast just south of Silkstream Junction. *Author's collection*

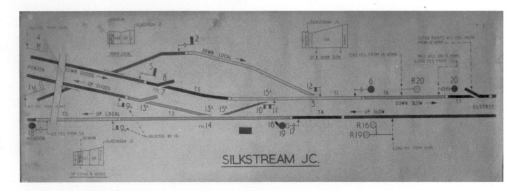

SILKSTREAM JC.

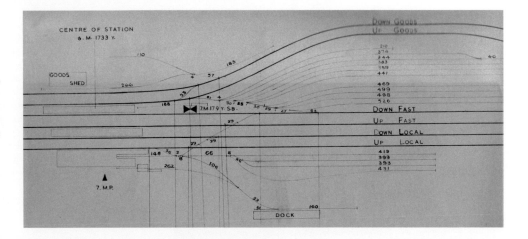

Above: **HENDON** signal box is seen here on 2 July 1977. Behind it can be seen the Goods lines, with the Fast lines in the foreground. The box had 65 levers, and closed on 26 April 1981.

Left: **HENDON** station opened with the line on 13 July 1868 (having opened to goods traffic on 9 March), and its four platforms are served today by Thameslink services. This official photograph records the removal of the arms from the Up Fast starting signal at the London end of the station on Sunday 26 April 1981, when the signal box closed and multiple-aspect colour signalling was introduced between here and Engine Shed Junction, Kentish Town. The overbridge carries Station Road. Signal WH32 will be operated by the new West Hampstead power signal box, which had come into operation in October 1979. Note immediately behind the head of the new colour signal is a shorter signal post on the bracket, which once held a 'splitting distant' signal arm for Welsh Harp Junction.

Between 1870 and 1903 there was a station at Welsh Harp, the locality named after a nearby pub of that name. A reservoir, fed by the River Brent and the Silk Stream, was built here in the 1830s to supply water to the Regent's and Grand Union canals, and it became a popular recreation venue, being then well outside London. Double junctions connected the Local and Fast lines, and separately the Fast and Goods lines, until abolished in 1967. *BR(LMR)*

BRENT JUNCTIONS After the line had crossed the 19-arch Brent Viaduct (at the present-day southern end of the M1 where it meets the North Circular Road at Staples Corner), it ran through the huge yards at Brent, laid out by the Midland on 150 acres of land acquired for the purpose, probably then the nearest open land to St Pancras and still farmland. The yards' purpose was to receive the enormous quantity of coal trains from the Derbyshire and Nottinghamshire coalfields sent south from Toton; at Brent the trains were remarshalled to distribute the vital cargo around the capital. The photograph is looking south across the complex on 30 June 1977, with Brent Junction No 2 signal box on the right nearer the camera, and No 1 box on the opposite side of the lines at milepost 6. A group of sidings on the down side (nearest the camera) were known as the Battersea Coal Sidings, giving an indication of the destination of the coal trains assembled there.

BRENT JUNCTIONS This was the view on Saturday 28 September 1974 from the front of a DMU approaching Brent Junction No 1 on the Up Local line — not a very good picture, but it does show some of the fine array of semaphore signals then still in use. All the Fast and Local signals are 'off' — was the box switched out?

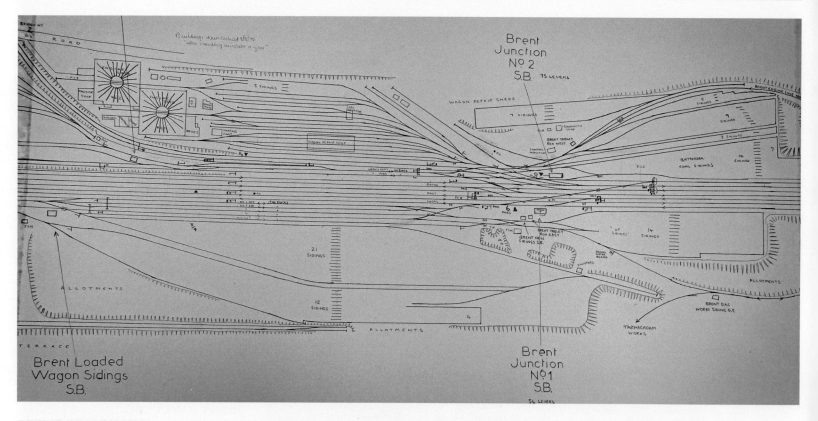

BRENT JUNCTIONS This map, based on a 1951 original, gives some idea of the size of the yards. Note at the right-hand perimeter the 'Engine Line', which went from one side of the complex to the other, ducking under the main line near Brent Viaduct, to enable engines to pass from the down side to the up (and vice versa) without crossing the main lines. The blocks of sidings on the up side (bottom of map) were the Brent Loaded Wagon Sidings, while those on the down side in the triangle of the Acton line junctions were, logically, the Brent Empty Wagon Sidings, no doubt mainly empty coal wagons waiting to return north to be filled.

Seen on the down side here (top left) are the two roundhouses and yard of Cricklewood shed (coded 14A), which opened in 1892. An important steam shed, it later became the principal diesel depot for supplying locomotives and DMUs to the southern end of the Midland Main Line; it closed in November 1964. Curving around the shed is the north-to-west chord of the triangular junction with the Acton branch, opened in 1884.

The site of the shed is now the Fellows Square apartment complex, and the Loaded Wagon Sidings area now accommodates the stabling and servicing area for Thameslink and East Midlands Railway trains on the site of the former diesel Traction Maintenance Depot. At the northern end of the site is the Hendon waste transfer station, which dispatches the 'Binliner' waste container trains to the landfill site at Calvert in Buckinghamshire. *Author*

Left: **BRENT JUNCTIONS** A closer view of Brent Junction No 1, on a rather sunnier 2 July 1977. The box had 56 levers, and closed on 23 July 1978.

Below: **BRENT JUNCTIONS** In the foreground is the rear of Brent Junction No 2 signal box, seen on 8 February 1975 from across the wasteland that had been the Battersea and Acton Branch sidings. Larger than No 1, it had 75 levers, and closed on 25 April 1981, when multiple-aspect signalling came into operation. Across the tracks is No 1 box. The foreground is now occupied by the Staples Corner Retail Park.

BRENT JUNCTIONS This pre-war OS maps shows Brent Empty Wagon Sidings in the triangle formed by the Acton Branch junctions. Bisecting the triangle is Edgware Road (or Watling Street, the A5) and the long-established Cricklewood bus garage, which was completely rebuilt in 2010. The 'Clock Works' were those of Smith's Industries, established in 1915 as S. Smith & Sons, making fuses, instruments and accessories; by the Second World War the company was making electric motors, aircraft accessories and electric clocks. Their advert on the 'Cricklewood Curve' railway bridge over Edgware Road was a familiar local landmark for many years. The 'Film Studios' dated from 1920 and were operated by Stoll Pictures during the silent film era through to 1938; at the time they were the largest film studios in the British Isles. Smith's is now a Wickes DIY store, and the studios are now a branch of Matalan.

Note the railway houses in the top right-hand corner, the terraces named after prominent Midland Railway officials, including Johnson, Needham, Campion and Gratton. *Crown Copyright*

BRENT JUNCTIONS On 8 February 1975 an oil train waits to leave the Up Acton branch as a 'Peak' (looks like a 'namer') passes on the Down Main line with a northbound passenger train. The wasteland in the foreground had once been the Wagon Repair Shop sidings and Cricklewood shed yard.

BRENT JUNCTIONS A similar view on the same day but without trains shows more clearly the fine semaphore signals, and the two signal boxes in the distance. The four signal arms in the centre controlled the exit from the Down Departure line to either the down sidings or out onto the Down Goods or Down Fast.

BRENT JUNCTIONS Seen from a DMU on the Up Local line on 2 July 1977 are the Brent starting signals and Cricklewood Junction distant signals for the Up Fast, and the distant signal on the Up Goods. The white hut is Brent Empty Sidings signal frame, with those sidings beyond. Curving down through the grassy cutting on the right is the Acton branch.

BRENT JUNCTIONS A little further along, here are the Cricklewood Junction starting signals on the Down Local and Down Fast, with the Brent Junction No 1 distant signals below. The chimneyed terraces on the right skyline are the Midland Railway housing off Edgware Road.

CRICKLEWOOD station opened on 2 May 1870 as Child's Hill & Cricklewood; more populous Child's Hill lay east of Cricklewood adjoining Hampstead Heath. The station, seen here in the centre right of this pre-war OS map, was renamed simply Cricklewood on 1 May 1903. The 'Aeroplane Works' (top left) were those of Handley Page, which had since 1912 been located in what became the Stoll film studios (see above). The company moved to Claremont Road in 1917, and between 1919 and 1929 Cricklewood Aerodrome was laid out adjacent to the factory, on what is now the Golders Green Estate. Some of the first flights between London and Paris flew from here; now, of course, one can catch a train to Paris from Cricklewood, via St Pancras International! *Crown Copyright*

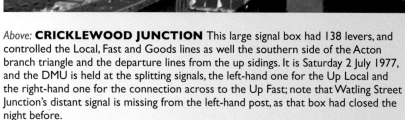

Above: **CRICKLEWOOD JUNCTION** This large signal box had 138 levers, and controlled the Local, Fast and Goods lines as well the southern side of the Acton branch triangle and the departure lines from the up sidings. It is Saturday 2 July 1977, and the DMU is held at the splitting signals, the left-hand one for the Up Local and the right-hand one for the connection across to the Up Fast; note that Watling Street Junction's distant signal is missing from the left-hand post, as that box had closed the night before.

The large buildings on the left are the Express Dairy, one of several rail-connected dairies operated by the company. The Express Country Milk Supply Company was established in London in 1864 by George Barham, becoming the Express Dairy Company Limited in 1892. The site of the dairy is now occupied by Dairyman Close!

Above right: **CRICKLEWOOD** This view from the country end of the Down Fast line platform dates from 29 June 1977. Another poor-quality picture, I'm afraid, but it shows that the connections to the Acton line to the left and across to the Down Local on the right have been taken out of use, and only a distant signal for Brent Junction No 2 survives. On the left the signals routing to the Acton line (left) and onto the Down Goods (right) are also out of use. Today there are no connections between any of the three pairs of tracks.

Right: **CRICKLEWOOD** On 2 July 1977 a red flag halts the progress of my northbound DMU in the Down Local line platform. This was a weekend of considerable signalling alterations. Various people are at work on the tracks, and the 'signalman' at the end of the platform seems to have a makeshift shelter while he is hand-signalling trains. The 'Cricklewood Curve' heads westwards towards Dudding Hill Junction and Acton in the middle distance.

Above: **CRICKLEWOOD** On the same day, here is a closer view of 'Cricklewood Curve'. The signals facing the camera control access to the Down Empty Wagon Reception line (the small arm on the left) and the Down Goods line (the large arm, with a 'calling-on' signal beneath). The bracket signal is the Up Goods home.

Right: **CRICKLEWOOD** Looking back towards the station from the 'Cricklewood Curve' on 8 February 1975, I photographed this delightful Midland Railway lower-quadrant signal controlling 'wrong line' reversing movements from the Down branch.

DUDDING HILL JUNCTION

DUDDING HILL JUNCTION lies at the western apex of the triangular junction from Brent Junction No 2 (the line on the left being taken by the freight train) and Cricklewood Junction (the line climbing slightly to the right); the lines run parallel for quite a distance before diverging at the back of Cricklewood bus garage. The box contained just 16 levers, and survives today on this now freight-only line. There was a passenger station here, variously named Willesden & Dudden Hill, then Dudding Hill (both during its opening year of 1875), Dudding Hill for Church End Willesden and Dudding Hill for Willesden & Neasden. It closed in 1902 – according to the excellent 'Disused Stations' website, the station had taken just under £2,000 in fares during its entire existence!

In the background is the gloriously ornate Cricklewood Pumping Station, which opened in 1905 to pump water from the Thames to supply London's north-western suburbs. The water was stored in reservoirs at Golders Green and Muswell Hill, among others. It was originally rail connected, and coal-fired until the 1950s; the now disused chimney has found a new use as mobile phone tower No 44933!

WATLING STREET JUNCTION South of Cricklewood the Midland Main Line turns eastward, skirting the high ground of Hampstead to the north. Between Cricklewood and West Hampstead stations was the intermediate signal box at Watling Street Junction. Residential development on this north-western edge of London was only beginning when the railway arrived, so the Roman Road of Watling Street – later the A5 and known here historically as Shoot Up Hill after a local farm – was probably the only local landmark when it came to naming the junction.

Looking back towards Cricklewood from Minster Road bridge on 19 September 1974, the layout is clearly seen as a St Pancras-bound DMU runs along the Up Fast towards signal No 48. The connection between the Up Local and Up Fast appears little used.

WATLING STREET JUNCTION By comparison, this was the scene on 12 July 1978. The signal box had closed on the night of Friday/Saturday 1/2 July 1977. The final Train Register Book, in the author's possession, records that at 23.35 on the Friday 'Up Local to Up Fast junction, Down Fast to Down Local junction clipped out of use pending removal.' At 01.10 on Saturday morning the Up Slow-Down Slow crossover was clipped out of use, as was the crossover from the 2nd Up Goods to Up Local. The signalman signed off duty at 06.00.

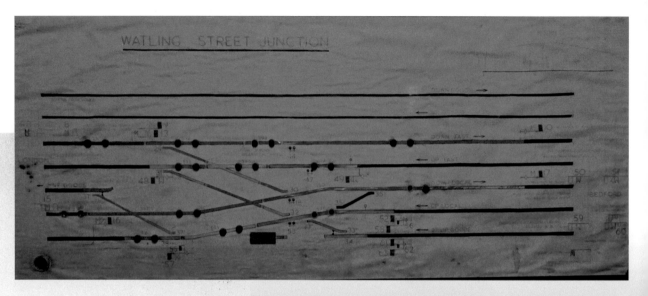

WATLING STREET JUNCTION

Above: **WATLING STREET JUNCTION** At this point there were in fact eight tracks: looking towards St Pancras, they were the 2nd Up Goods, Up and Down Local, Up and Down Fast, Up and Down Goods, and 2nd Down Goods, and all were controlled by Watling Street. However, by the time of closure, as this picture of the final signal box diagram shows, only seven remained, the 2nd Down Goods having been removed; also, the Goods lines were no longer under the control of the box, and a former double-line connection between the Goods and Fast lines has also gone. Of note is the 2nd Up Goods, which crossed the Local lines here to continue towards West Hampstead between the Local and Fast lines – it was a kind of second, elongated, crossover between the Local and Fast lines, capable of holding a complete train. *Author's collection*

Left: **WATLING STREET JUNCTION** On Sunday 2 July 1977 the box is closed and all the semaphore signal arms have been removed. Note the white painted square on Minster Road bridge to aid sighting of the West Hampstead distant arm below signal No 48 against the brickwork. This bridge, No 39, was demolished and rebuilt in 1979.

WATLING STREET JUNCTION Looking towards West Hampstead on 19 September 1974, a 'Peak'-hauled train approaches the Watling Street home signals controlling the Fast to Local junction; it is signalled through to Cricklewood. In the background is the mighty Mill Lane overbridge. The 2nd Up Goods diverges from the Local lines on the left to run between the Local and Fast lines towards West Hampstead, round the corner.

WATLING STREET JUNCTION This is the same signal on 30 June 1977. Note that the Cricklewood distant arm for the Down Fast has disappeared, and other signals will disappear within days with the closure of the box. Note the new colour-light signal on the Down Goods, with its 'feather' indicators providing plenty of warning for the new replacement 'ladder' junction connecting the lines between here and Cricklewood. The grassy area used to accommodate the shunting neck for West End Sidings.

Right: **WEST END SIDINGS** were located on the down side of the line between Watling Street and West Hampstead. Until 1968 the sidings had their own signal box, controlling connections to the Goods lines only, at the Cricklewood end (note the Mill Lane overbridge at the extreme right of the plan). West Hampstead station opened on 1 March 1871 as 'West End', then the name of the village, hence the sidings' name. The sidings were used for general merchandise, and could accommodate 900 wagons; as this 1949 plan shows, three sidings were used by the North Metropolitan Power Company for coal traffic (the area adjacent to Maygrove Road was occupied by a coal wharf). The sidings closed in the late 1960s, then in 1973 14 acres of the derelict land were bought by Camden Council to become the West End Estate of council housing and a school, built between 1978 and 1982. *Author's collection*

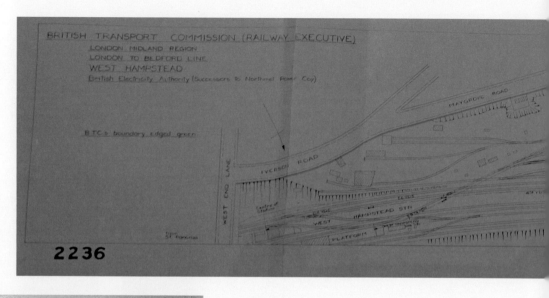

Left: **WEST HAMPSTEAD** When the Midland opened in 1868 there was no station here in the village of West End until 'West End for Kilburn and Hampstead' (the MR spreading its net wide!) in 1871. In 1903 it became just West End, then in 1904 'and Brondesbury' was added before the station became West Hampstead in 1905. 'Midland' was added to the name in 1950, replaced by 'Thameslink' in 1988.

This view across the country end of the station on 19 September 1974 shows the long central platform serving the Down Local and Up Fast lines; note how much shorter the Down Fast platform is (right foreground), although it extends further at the London end. There were no platforms on the Goods lines. There is a fine Midland Railway bracket signal in the foreground, with more recent upper-quadrant arms; the taller post has an MR lower-quadrant 'shunt ahead' subsidiary arm below it.

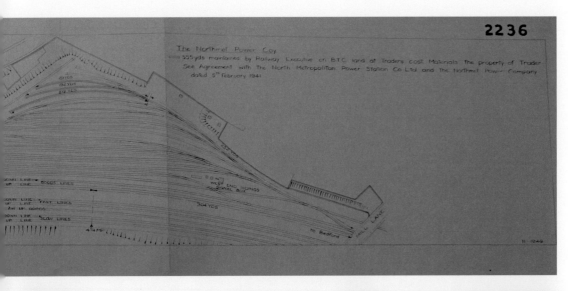

2236

The Northmet Power Coy
555yds maintained by Railway Executive on B.T.C. land at Traders cost Materials the property of Trader
See Agreement with The North Metropolitan Power Station Co Ltd and The Northmet Power Company
dated 5th February 1941

WEST HAMPSTEAD A DMU stands at the Down Fast Platform 4 on 2 July 1977, the weekend of signalling alterations; there appears to be a flagman at the end of the platform. Note that the Goods line signal on the right has lost the 'shunt ahead' arm but has gained a distant arm for Cricklewood, and the Down Goods to Down Fast signal has been removed, the connection having presumably been take out of use. It looks as though building materials have arrived for the new power signal box across the lines from the mechanical box.

WEST HAMPSTEAD's up home signals are seen from Black Path, a footpath running parallel with the up side of the station, on 19 September 1974. This was a good place from which to watch the trains, as in the summer when the windows were open one could hear the telegraph bell signals! On the left is the Up Local home and Finchley Road outer distant. The two small arms in the centre are at the end of the 2nd Up Goods from Watling Street, indicating the two routes to the Up Fast and Up Goods; until 1970 there had been a third connection to the Up Local. The bracket signal is for the Up Fast (cleared for the 'Peak'-hauled train) and Up Fast to Up Goods, with Finchley Road distants. On the right can just be seen the Up Goods home.

    Today the former 2nd Up Goods still exists, but is now simply a loop line leaving the Down Local at West Hampstead and rejoining it just west of the former Watling Street Junction.

WEST HAMPSTEAD signal box is seen from the end of Platform 2. The fine signal is the Down Local starter No 14 above the Watling Street Junction Down Local distant No 15.

Right: **WEST HAMPSTEAD** Seen from Iverson Road on 5 June 1977, work is about to begin on the power signal box. It was brought into use in stages between 1979 and 1982.

Below: **WEST HAMPSTEAD** signal box closed on 29 April 1978, and by 12 July it stands empty, the block shelf apparently devoid of instruments and the nameboard gone. The semaphore signal has been replaced by a colour light, which will be operated from the new power signal box that is taking shape across the tracks.

Below: **WEST HAMPSTEAD** This more distant view on the same day gives a better impression of the new power box. The sawn-off post of the semaphore signal is silhouetted against the wall of the box. Some work is being done on the platform.

WEST HAMPSTEAD This photograph is dated 30 July 1979, and shows the reconstruction of Bridge 36 (West End Lane), involving the demolition of the decrepit and smoke-stained Midland Parade shops as part of the ongoing electrification works. The bridge in the distance, carrying the North London Line over the Midland, is also in the process of reconstruction. *BR(LMR)*

WEST HAMPSTEAD A DMU calls at the Up Local platform on 19 September 1974. The entrance to the station is at the left-hand end of the footbridge in a rather temporary-looking structure, presumably having replaced a more substantial booking office. The road overbridge carries West End Lane and a row of single-storey shops, which were known as Midland Parade. When the station opened in 1871 the entrance was on the opposite side of the lines in Iverson Road, with access again by footbridge; strangely, the present-day access is once again in Iverson Road, via a new building and two footbridges, one incorporating passenger lifts.

Finchley Road

Right: **FINCHLEY ROAD** This 1968 diagram of the junctions at Finchley Road shows that the Local (here labelled Slow) and Fast lines converge to become the Up and Down Passenger lines using Belsize New Tunnel, while the Goods lines use the original tunnel. The North London line from West End Lane towards Hampstead Heath crosses here, with a footpath beside it. A few hundred yards to the south (beyond the sidings at the top of the plan) run the Jubilee and Metropolitan lines, and the former Great Central line into Marylebone – effectively five railways running more or less parallel within a quarter of a mile. The Midland and Metropolitan lines were connected by intermediate exchange sidings. Note that Cadbury's had a depot here.

Below right: **FINCHLEY ROAD** This is the North London Line bridge in the course of being rebuilt on 20 January 1980, looking towards West Hampstead. A footpath, which runs from West End Lane to Lithos Road, was also incorporated on the near side of the bridge – in 2011 this path was christened Billy Fury Way in recognition of the fact that the rock'n'roll star recorded regularly at Decca Studios in Broadhurst Gardens, on the far side of the Metropolitan/GCR lines.

Inset above: The same bridge as it appeared in Williams's *Midland Railway* in 1876.

BRIDGE UNDER HAMPSTEAD JUNCTION.

FINCHLEY ROAD This was the view from the future Billy Fury Way on 19 September 1974 as a 'Peak' 'namer' heads towards St Pancras on the Up Fast. In the foreground we see the rears of the Finchley Road down starters with the West Hampstead inner distants below them. There used to be a couple of sidings on the extreme left, and the down sidings and coal yard on the right are clearly still in use at this date. The splitting down home signal for the divergence of the Fast and Local lines beyond the box is already a colour-light, which would aid sighting from within the tunnel.

FINCHLEY ROAD By 20 January 1980 the removal of mechanical signalling on the Fast and Local lines allows a clearer view of the layout. Only the Goods lines still have semaphore signals, and there is no physical connection between the passenger and freight lines (there used to be a trailing crossover between Down Fast and Up Goods nearer the signal box). The goods yard is still in use, and would remain so until May 1983. Finchley Road signal box closed on 25 April 1981 with the introduction of multiple-aspect signalling.

On the 'peninsula' between the two lines can be seen some large buildings – these are all that remained of Finchley Road station (briefly '& St Johns Wood'), which was located on the Passenger line between the signal box and the mouth of Belsize New Tunnel. It had opened with the railway in 1868, outside the original Belsize Tunnel on what became the Goods lines, but in 1884, with the completion of the New Tunnel, the station was moved across to the new Passenger lines. The station was accessed down steps from Finchley Road through a gateway flanked by small offices and shops known as Midland Crescent. The station suffered from road competition, and the LMS closed it on 11 July 1927, and there are few traces today.

Interestingly, now that goods traffic movement is no longer of importance, today's layout has the Fast lines slewed across to the Goods line side to use the original tunnel once more, leaving the New Tunnel for Thameslink services. What were the Goods lines are connected to the modern-day Fast lines by a single turnout.

Right: **FINCHLEY ROAD**
A sketch map based on a 1951 official plan showing the remains of Finchley Road station. *Author*

Below: **FINCHLEY ROAD**
Looking from above the old Belsize Tunnel on 5 September 1976, this is the site of the original Finchley Road station. The arched doorway on the extreme right led to a footbridge that spanned the tracks before the platforms were moved in 1884.

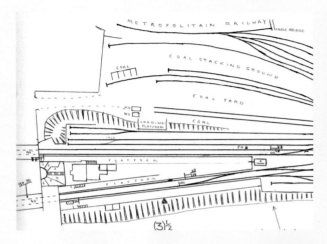

Below: **FINCHLEY ROAD** This is the mouth of the original Belsize Tunnel on the same day. It is 1,707 (or 1,734, depending on source) yards long, and the first brick was ceremonially laid on 27 January 1865, the last on 20 June 1867. With two passenger lines and two goods lines reduced to a single pair of lines through the tunnel, it inevitably became a bottleneck, so as part of the Midland's ongoing widening works along the London extension, a new tunnel was built and opened in 1884, 1,619 (or 1,822) yards long. Old maps show that, when built, the mouth of the old tunnel, then out in the country, was on the east side of Finchley Road, but this was subsequently covered by housing development. The distant signal is for Carlton Road Junction, more than a mile away; it repeats a colour light signal within the tunnel.

CARLTON ROAD JUNCTION On leaving the Belsize Tunnels the erstwhile Passenger and Goods lines enter deep brick-lined cuttings, making the route difficult to photograph. Immediately outside the eastern portal was Haverstock Hill station, which opened with the line in 1868 and was remodelled when the second tunnel was added in 1884. It was intended to serve a proposed residential development around Lismore Circus, but this did not happen as envisaged, growing road transport began to eat into revenues, and the station closed on 1 January 1916; the station's signal box closed in 1946. Some evidence of the cut-back platforms can still be seen.

After passing through a section of covered way, the line entered a junction complex on two levels before arriving at Kentish Town station. This is the view looking back towards the junction from the rear of a DMU on the Down Passenger on 8 May 1976. The signalling through the Haverstock Hill cuttings was multiple-aspect by this time, but it can be seen that some mechanical signalling survived here. The tracks diverging to the left are the Tottenham North Curve round to Mortimer Street Junction (of which more shortly) and the Slow lines, which use the tunnel to the left of the signal box and reinstate three pairs of lines once more. As can be seen, the Tottenham line connected with both the Passenger and Goods lines. Crossing the Midland above the short tunnels in the distance is the North London Line.

Carlton Road Junction signal box, a BR-built structure dating from the 1960s, closed on 22 October 1978; parts of it were subsequently used to build a new box at Uttoxeter, which opened in 1981. The site is now occupied by a relay room for West Hampstead power signal box.

CARLTON ROAD JUNCTION This later view from 27 May 1979, taken from bridge No 25 carrying Grafton Road – formerly Carlton Road – shows that all connections with what had been the Goods line, but is now the Passenger/Fast line, have been removed, and the pointwork cut back; today the connection from the still extant Tottenham line is further west by a 'ladder' junction. This view gives a slightly better view of Tottenham North Curve Tunnel No 1, and the diverging Slow line going round the back of the box. The Midland Railway just squeezed past the building on the right!

CARLTON ROAD JUNCTION This the view (not a good one, I'm afraid) looking west on 17 July 1977.

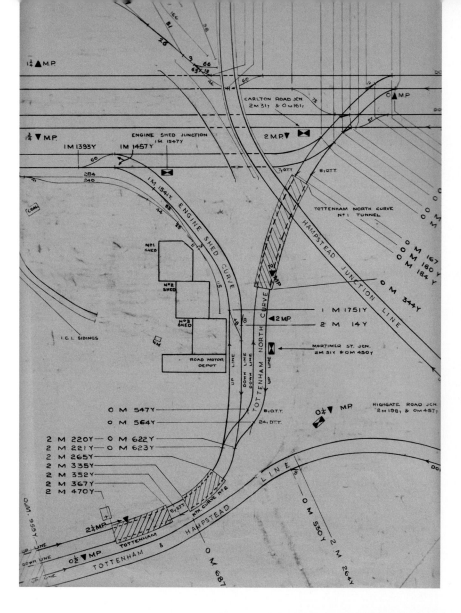

KENTISH TOWN JUNCTIONS This BR plan (south at the top) shows the layout of the junctions west of Kentish Town in 1968. Carlton Road Junction is top right, where the two pairs of tracks become three again. At the northern apex of the 'ground level' triangle (centre) is Mortimer Street Junction, and at the third, eastern, apex is Engine Shed Junction.

The trackless bridge across the Midland indicates the route of the former upper-level link – the Tottenham South Curve – from Kentish Town Junction, which crossed the main line parallel with the Hampstead Junction line (North London Railway) and joined the Tottenham & Hampstead line at Highgate Road Junction and (high level) station; this connection opened in 1870 and in 1902 became joint MR/GER property. As Williams put it in 1876, 'by this means access is obtained to several suburbs of interest in the north of London, and also, via Stratford, to the Victoria Docks, and to the Great Eastern Railway generally.' In 1894 the Tottenham & Forest Gate Railway linked this line with the London, Tilbury & Southend Railway (which was vested in the MR from 1912); excursions to Southend and Tilbury boat trains used this route until 1963, and it closed the following year.

Meanwhile, down below, the Tottenham North Curve once had a low-level Highgate Road station, before rising to meet the upper-level line at the delightfully named Junction Road Junction. Note that the yards outside the three Kentish Town roundhouses have been erased; the shed, coded 14B, closed in April 1963.
Author's collection

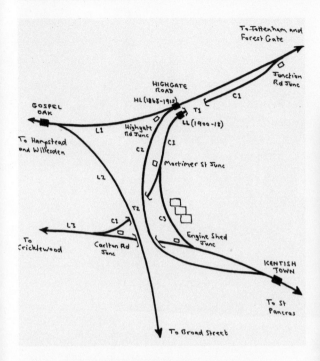

KENTISH TOWN JUNCTIONS A sketch map showing the layout of the junctions at their fullest extent.

Key
C1 Tottenham North Curve
C2 Tottenham South Curve
C3 Engine Shed Curve

L1 Tottenham & Hampstead line
L2 Hampstead Junction line
L3 Midland Main Line

T1 Tottenham North Curve Tunnel No 2
T2 Tottenham North Curve Tunnel No 1

MORTIMER STREET JUNCTION This is the mouth of the 160-yard-long Tottenham North Curve Tunnel No 1, looking towards Carlton Road Junction on 10 July 1977, with Mortimer Street's down starter above the Carlton Road distants (one out of shot to the left); these distants were only the tunnel's length from the home signals, but trains would have been travelling slowly round the curve.

MORTIMER STREET JUNCTION This unusual signal box had a particular attraction for me, so much so that when in 1977 the Victorian Society announced a measured drawing competition, I entered and submitted a set of drawings of the box. I didn't win anything, but it enabled me to get permission from the authorities to visit the box for purposes of measuring it up and photographing it (it was otherwise pretty inaccessible).

We are now looking north past the box towards the apex of the triangular junction. The box was elevated and dug into the cutting side. On the right is the wall of Kentish Town shed's No 3 roundhouse, and in the distance above the retaining wall are the arches that carried the Tottenham South Curve to Highgate Road Junction.

Above: **MORTIMER STREET JUNCTION** We are now looking along Engine Shed Curve towards Mortimer Street on 9 July 1978, with the former loco shed buildings much in evidence. The signal is the down home from Engine Shed Junction, No 27.

Right: **MORTIMER STREET JUNCTION** This is the view in the opposite direction on the same day. In the distance is Engine Shed Junction signal box, which controlled the junction with the Slow lines of the main line, while on the left is No 1 roundhouse of Kentish Town shed. Until 1964 there was an additional line on the left giving access to the 'City Carriage Sidings' and the shed yard, both adjacent to the main line. Strangely, Engine Shed Junction did not control access to the shed, but was merely adjacent to it; Kentish Town Sidings box performed that function (until closure in September 1969). The area on the right once accommodated four carriage sidings controlled by Mortimer Street. Prior to the introduction of the electric multiple unit services there was a half-hourly service from Kentish Town to Barking, using this line, after which trains from Barking were diverted to Gospel Oak. Engine Shed Curve has since closed, and the Junction Road to Carlton Road line realigned to obliterate any sign of Mortimer Street Junction.

Left: **MORTIMER STREET JUNCTION** signal box was elevated above the tracks, so that the point rodding had to be carried down to track level by means of cranks, and the signal wires by pulleys.

Below: **MORTIMER STREET JUNCTION** Some of the cranks and rodding can be seen on the left. As well as the steps up to the box, there was a flight of steps down to track level. Note the bicycle frame hanging on the wall of the lavatory extension!

MORTIMER STREET JUNCTION This was the signal box diagram on closure, with no sign of the sidings that had been controlled by levers 12 to 20 and 24. *Author's collection*

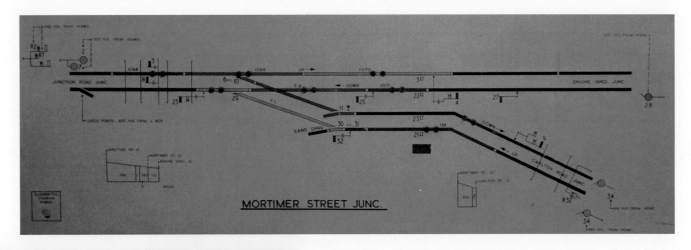

MORTIMER STREET JUNC.

MORTIMER STREET JUNCTION The interior of the box. The frame had 34 levers, and the white-painted levers towards the centre of the frame were those made redundant when the connections to the shed and the carriage sidings were removed in 1964. The armchair perhaps indicates a not-very-busy box!

MORTIMER STREET JUNCTION This is the view from the box looking north on 17 July 1977. Just beyond the junction is the Highgate Road overbridge, then the entrance to Tottenham North Curve Tunnel No 2, the line then rising at 1 in 100 towards Junction Road Junction. Note how the arms of the down starting signal are tucked into the recess in the retaining wall. Somehow in 1900 the Midland squeezed Highgate Road Low Level station into the space between the junction and the tunnel, but it closed on 1 March 1918. High Level station was directly above, on the viaduct.

MORTIMER STREET JUNCTION Here's a similar view from track level on 9 July 1978. Note the semaphore signal on the high-level Tottenham & Hampstead line.

MORTIMER STREET JUNCTION In this view looking along the signal box's access path from Mortimer Terrace (not 'Street', strangely) on 17 July 1977, the splitting distants for Carlton Road can be seen by the tunnel, together with the flight of steps from the box to track level. The building work on the left is on the site of Kentish Town shed's Road Motor Depot and smithy, adjacent to No 3 roundhouse, and is now a small residential estate.

Incidentally, in pre-railway days the poet John Keats lived for a while in the newly built Mortimer Terrace (named after a farmer of that name).

MORTIMER STREET JUNCTION A year later, on 9 July 1978, the signals at the tunnel mouth have disappeared, and the box has only just over three months left. The buildings on the left are nearly finished.

Above left and above: **MORTIMER STREET JUNCTION** signal box closed on 22 October 1978, and by 27 May 1979 had been demolished. No semaphores are visible, and a colour light signal now controls the tunnelled approach to Carlton Road Junction.

Left: **MORTIMER STREET JUNCTION** Looking north towards the junction the down home signal survives – but worked by whom?

HIGHGATE ROAD HIGH LEVEL This is the site of the station, looking towards Junction Road Junction on 17 July 1977. The girders of the bridge over Highgate Road can just be seen, across which the platforms extended. The station opened on 21 July 1868, and closed on 1 October 1915. The junction signal box closed in 1965 following closure of the Tottenham South Curve to Kentish Town the previous year.

Incidentally, Junction Road's name has nothing to do with railways. It was constructed in 1813 as a feeder between the new Archway Road and Kentish Town, and later featured cheap housing for working people who had been displaced by the Midland Railway's arrival at St Pancras. Junction Road station opened in 1872 and saw its last train on 3 May 1943. The fact that the junction was logically named Junction Road Junction presumably didn't faze the straight-faced Midland and T&H directors! The signal box closed on 10 November 1985.

ENGINE SHED JUNCTION signal box is seen on 10 July 1977 from on top of the short tunnel above the Midland Main Line across which the North London Line ran. In the foreground are the remains of the Tottenham South Curve bridge; the line it carried originated at Kentish Town Junction (closed in 1969), which was located just this side of the right-hand end of the overbridge in the distance, beyond which is Kentish Town station. The line from Mortimer Street Junction is coming in beyond the box, and the area on the left was once the yard of Kentish Town shed, but for many years has been the main depot of civil engineers J. Murphy & Sons. Backing onto the yard was Read Brothers Brewery, seen in many photographs of locomotives on shed. The large building in the centre skyline was built in 1934 as an art deco cinema. It then became an Irish dance hall and a bingo hall, then in the 1980s a live music venue, the Town & Country Club. Its last act was Van Morrison in 1993, then it was purchased by Mean Fiddler. In 2007 it was extensively renovated and since 2015 has been the O_2 Forum Kentish Town, as part of the O_2 Academy Group.

Engine Shed Junction box closed on 6 December 1981 when West Hampstead power box took over signalling in this area; it had the distinction of being the last Midland Railway mechanical box to be closed in connection with the Midland line electrification.

ENGINE SHED JUNCTION Another view of the Tottenham South Curve bridge being dismantled a week later on 17 July 1977.

At Kentish Town the line swung southwards. **Kentish Town station** opened with the Midland line in 1868 and had four platform faces, serving the Slow and Fast Lines; the Goods lines were added with the 1884 widening, and had no platforms. By contrast, today's arrangement is almost the opposite: there are now no dedicated goods lines, and the former Goods lines are now the through fast lines, still with no platforms. The other platforms are used by Thameslink services.

The route now runs through deep blue-brick cuttings, and by the early 1970s was controlled principally by multiple-aspect signalling, which for me was less photogenic, and in any case the locations were pretty inaccessible for photography.

Just beyond Kentish Town was **Islip Street Junction** (named after the road crossing the railway at this point by bridge No 19. This area was developed by the landowner, Christ Church, Oxford, in the 1860s, and Gillian Tindall – see the Bibliography – suggests that they knew of the railway's coming and reckoned they would make more money if the railway had to purchase and demolish houses rather than simply purchase open fields!). This junction provided connections between the various lines. The signal box was damaged by fire at the end of 1966 and not replaced.

Shortly afterwards came **Camden Road station**, which opened in 1868 and, like Kentish Town, had four platforms, with access from Camden Road above. It closed as a First World War economy measure on New Year's Day 1916, and never reopened. Traces survived until the 1960s, but there's little to be seen today other than marks in the brickwork.

There then follows a covered way of about 300 yards beneath Camden Square, known as Camden Road Tunnels, before the railway emerged at the St Paul's Road junctions.

ST PAUL'S ROAD GOODS signal box controlled only the Goods lines and the entrance to St Pancras Goods Station. This view, looking across the few remaining lines into the goods station site, was taken on 21 February 1976, as a 'Peak'-hauled train approaches St Pancras on what were then the Fast lines. The bridge (No 14) carries Agar Grove, which was formerly St Paul's Road but was renamed in the early 20th century after William Agar, who was landlord of the notorious 1840s slums of Agar Town, a squalid settlement swept away by the coming of the railway. The Goods box was out of use at this time, having closed the previous December.

Beyond the bridge on the up side was St Paul's Road Passenger signal box, controlling the Slow and Fast lines, and just beyond it the Moorgate line (now Thameslink) started to descend into St Pancras Tunnel, which passed beneath the terminus to join the 'Widened Lines' at King's Cross; it now passes through the subterranean 'box' of St Pancras Thameslink station. Attached to the retaining wall here was a '0' milepost headed 'SPR' – St Pancras Railway. This box had closed as long ago as 1956, just prior to the St Pancras resignalling scheme of 1958, of which more shortly.

In 2014 the same location is very different. This is the view looking north from the footpath that parallels the North London Line bridge across the Midland – St Paul's Road Goods box would have stood somewhere near the last relay cabinets on the left, and the much-graffitied buildings on the left cover the throat of the former goods station. Although there are still four tracks here, it is the middle two that appear to be the principal lines; the lines down to the subsurface St Pancras Thameslink platforms A and B, then on to Blackfriars and all points south, start their descent on the right.

Below left: **DOCK JUNCTION** After passing beneath the North London Line (again), the next signal box was Dock Junction, which controlled a trailing connection between Cambridge Street siding and a down carriage siding across to the Down Passenger and Down Goods lines. *The Railway Magazine* of November 1956 reported that 'St Pancras is one of the few terminal stations in London still equipped with mechanical signalling, and a modernisation scheme, which includes electro-pneumatic operation of points, combined with colour-light signals, controlled from a "panel"-type relay interlocking signal box, is now in progress. A certain amount of new work is being carried out between the terminus and Kentish Town…' Part of that involved the box seen here, which was brought into use on 27 May 1956, replacing a Midland Railway box that had stood immediately to the left of it.

An event that nearly ended the box's short life occurred on 20 July 1959 when the driver of 'Jubilee' No 45730 *Ocean* overran signals on the down carriage line and collided tender-first with the box. Hand signalling was in force in and out of St Pancras for several days while the box was repaired; it eventually closed on 15 July 1979.

DOCK JUNCTION AND NORTH LONDON INCLINE

This rather scruffy BR plan shows Dock Junction on the up side just beyond the irregularly shaped bridge carrying the North London Line, and on the down side, a little nearer St Pancras, North London Incline ground frame, controlling access to the single line that linked the Midland Goods line with the North London Line at Maiden Lane Junction (bottom right). The extent of the sidings in and around the Goods Station and across the Regent's Canal to further warehouses can be seen, even as late as 1968, the date of this plan.

Note that the Midland elected to cross the Regent's Canal, which resulted in the tracks arriving at the St Pancras buffer stops, on a falling gradient, some 16ft 6in above street level. Next door, the Great Northern had burrowed beneath the canal, thus arriving on Euston Road at street level, but necessitating sharp gradients beyond the canal tunnel heading north.
Author's collection

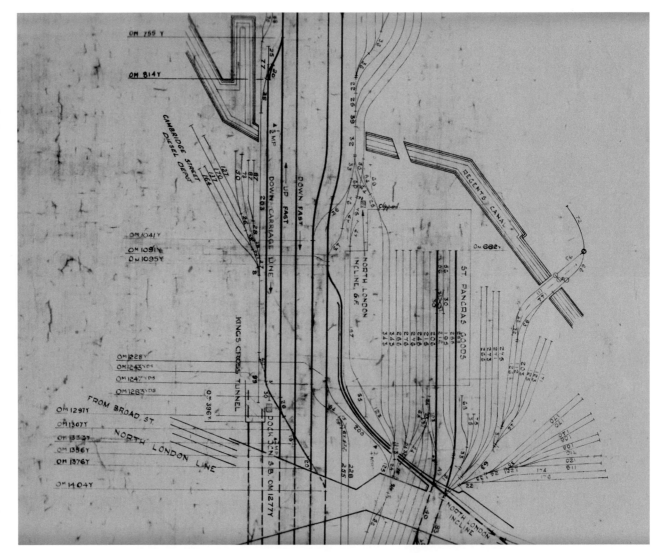

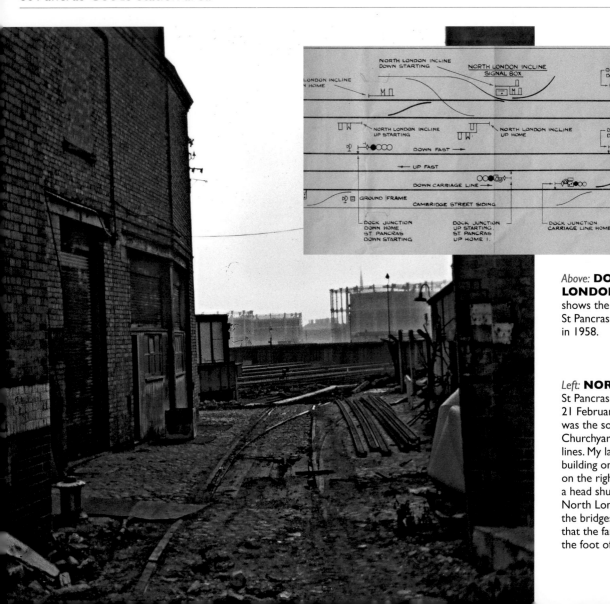

Above: **DOCK JUNCTION AND NORTH LONDON INCLINE** This rather clearer plan shows the two signal boxes as part of the St Pancras resignalling scheme ten years earlier, in 1958.

Left: **NORTH LONDON INCLINE** Most of St Pancras Goods Station had been demolished by 21 February 1976, the date of this photograph. This was the southern exit from the depot towards Churchyard Sidings on the down side of the Goods lines. My large-scale 1951 plan indicates that the building on the left was a sub-station, with a mess on the right; the track diverging to the right was a head shunt. Just glimpsed through the opening is North London Incline Frame, then the girders of the bridges across the Regent's Canal, and beyond that the famous gasholders. Note the capstan at the foot of the left-hand wall.

Below: **NORTH LONDON INCLINE** A closer view of the cobbled exit from the Goods Station and the rear of the ground frame on the same day. Beyond it a couple of 'Peaks' can be glimpsed in the Cambridge Street diesel stabling and refuelling point on the up side of the running lines. The depot opened in 1961, the year after St Pancras became fully dieselised (although steam still had to be called upon to cover early failures), and closed in 1984.

Right: **NORTH LONDON INCLINE** The nameboard is almost too big for the box! The earlier North London Incline signal box had stood a little to the north against the outside wall of the Goods Station, but a 'lever cabin' is marked at this point on my 1951 plan. The signal box closed at the end of 1961, when it was presumably replaced by this ground frame of 15 levers. This controlled a double-line connection with the Goods line, and via the Down Goods to the incline, but the points in the Goods line had to be released by Dock Junction prior to any movement.

Below: **NORTH LONDON INCLINE** The incline up to the North London Line was carried on a series of ten curving arches, then girders spanning the northern entrance to the Goods Station. According to my detailed 1951 plan, the arches were occupied by (lowest to highest) Rat catcher, Stores (2), Engineers, Carriage & Wagon, Mess (2), Workshop, Mess, and Locker Room. (A photo of 1953 shows rat-catchers Jim Forty and Alfred Greenwin with their dogs Jill, Sally and Tiny at St Pancras Goods Station.) Two of the arches are seen here, the left-hand one (with its bricked-up window) apparently boasting a chimney (one of the messes?). Above, it can be seen that there was a 5mph speed limit for the descent of the incline, together with the instruction 'Goods trains to stop…', with, it appears, further words missing beneath. A lean-to bike shed completes the picture.

Right: **NORTH LONDON INCLINE** Inside this arch (the workshop?) were the bellows for a forge and a huge number of iron tools and other items, including a large pillar drill.

Below: **NORTH LONDON INCLINE** A year later, on 11 February 1977, the incline is in the course of demolition – the partly felled girder section can be seen on the left.

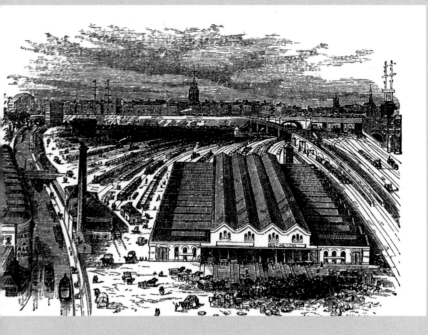

Below: **ST PANCRAS GOODS STATION** This was all that remained of that building just over a century later on 21 February 1976. The surviving structure on the extreme right is the right-hand ridge-roofed part of the goods station as seen in the engraving. In the distance can be seen the girder bridge carrying the North London Incline.

Above: **ST PANCRAS GOODS STATION** This engraving appears in Williams's *Midland Railway: Its Rise and Progress.* The Goods Station was authorised in 1860 and opened in 1865, before the main line reached the passenger station. The main line is on the right (with Dock Junction signal box just visible on the extreme right), and the North London Incline can clearly be seen (the ground frame would be in the bottom right-hand corner). The North London crosses right to left, and on the left is the Regent's Canal, with a bridge across from the goods yard to the Bass beer warehouse erected for the company by the Midland Railway. According to my 1951 plan, the chimney belonged to an incinerator. The goods station building contained a dozen tracks with cartways and a large number of cranes, mostly 25-ton, while outside (on the left) was a fan of 17 sidings as well as the lines across the canal.

ST PANCRAS GOODS STATION Looking from the bridge
across the canal that formed the Camley Street entrance to the
Goods Station, the Bass warehouse survives on the left, with bridge
No 10 connecting it to the main yard. Halfway down the building
there appears to be a covered wharf. By 1877 Bass of Burton-upon-
Trent had become the largest brewery in the world, with an annual
output of one million barrels. Naturally it used the Midland Railway
to deliver its products to London, although initially, in 1865, the
beer was delivered by canal. When the Midland opened for goods
traffic in September 1867, the beer began to arrive by rail. In 1871
Bass sent 238,880 barrels to St Pancras, some 36 per cent of its
annual output for the year. By 1874 Bass was dispatching about
150 wagons full of beer, and the canal-side warehouse could hold
100,000 36-gallon barrels in 6 acres of storage space; in that year
the brewery sold 292,306 barrels of beer in London, an average
daily delivery rate of 800 barrels. The warehouse employed 150
men, breaking down wooden hogsheads, each containing 54 gallons,
into smaller casks and bottles for delivery to pubs. When St Pancras
station opened in 1868 the operation was moved to the cellars
there, as we shall see.

In 2014 *(left)* redevelopment of the area is well under way. All the old
railway buildings have gone, to be replaced by modern office buildings.
Camley Street now runs right through the complex of domestic and
commercial buildings and under the North London Line, almost as far
as Agar Grove.

Left: **ST PANCRAS GOODS STATION** At the north end of the yard on 21 February 1976 we see the final girders of the incline as a train passes beyond on the North London Line. Through the bridge there's a glimpse of St Paul's Road Goods signal box. Note the two-lever ground frame in the foreground.

Bottom left: This is more or less the same view today. The North London Incline has now been replaced by bridges carrying new chord lines connecting the North London with St Pancras International and HS2.

Below: On the new Camley Street the abutment of bridge No 12, which carried the North London Line over the Midland yard, still carries its identifying bridge plate, alongside the more modern one for the new chord lines.

Right: **ST PANCRAS GOODS STATION** We are now looking into the site of the goods station from beneath the North London Line bridge and, just beyond it, the top of the North London Incline. The surviving portion of the depot is glimpsed on the left.

Left: **ST PANCRAS GOODS STATION** Just round the corner from the bridge was this grounded carriage body, being used a mess room – an early LMS corridor vehicle? Above the right-hand end can be seen the roof of a building identified on my 1951 plan as the Yard Inspector's office.

ST PANCRAS GOODS STATION Looking through and out from the remaining part of the goods depot on 21 February 1976, the arches beneath the North London Incline can be seen leading up to the four girder spans. This part of the building was largely occupied by a cartway with loading areas and cranes on the left, communicating through the arches with the depot proper. On the right was a single track serving a 'Passenger Parcels Loading Platform'.

St Pancras station

Right: **ST PANCRAS** We have now reached the terminus, and this photograph was taken from the rear of a DMU leaving the station on 8 May 1976. We are travelling on the 'East Departure', which shortly becomes the Down Fast line, joined by the 'West Departure' line on the right; out of sight on the right are the Goods lines, which used to serve Somers Town Goods Station, across Midland Road (so named in 1885), now the site of the British Library.

A little way behind the camera, south of the canal crossing, was Cambridge Street signal box, where the line crossed that street. At some point in the 1950s Cambridge Street's name was changed by the LCC to Camley Street, for reasons I have been unable to discover. Here were coal chutes on the up side, on Cambridge Street, together with a loco yard and turntable. (There were more coal chutes on the down side, at Churchyard Sidings, on Pancras Road.) Then came the famous gasholders, seen here on the extreme left. The 'Peak' is on the Up Fast, with the more distant one in Table Sidings (which also included a turntable). The bridge girders are those of Bridge No 1, over Pancras Road.

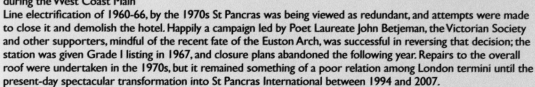

Left: **ST PANCRAS** The greatest transformation affecting the Midland Main Line in London has been that of St Pancras station itself. Despite modernisation of the layout and signalling in 1958, and its use as an alternative terminus during the West Coast Main Line electrification of 1960-66, by the 1970s St Pancras was being viewed as redundant, and attempts were made to close it and demolish the hotel. Happily a campaign led by Poet Laureate John Betjeman, the Victorian Society and other supporters, mindful of the recent fate of the Euston Arch, was successful in reversing that decision; the station was given Grade I listing in 1967, and closure plans abandoned the following year. Repairs to the overall roof were undertaken in the 1970s, but it remained something of a poor relation among London termini until the present-day spectacular transformation into St Pancras International between 1994 and 2007.

This photograph, taken on 8 May 1976, symbolises the old St Pancras in its 'wilderness years' – the old maroon and cream LMR enamel running-in board, a chimney from one of the premises beneath the station on Pancras Road, and the famous gasholders.

ST PANCRAS This BR plan shows the situation in 1968, when Somers Town Goods Station was still functioning, as seen on the right of the map. The depot was built on a 14-acre site beside the station on Euston Road between 1883 and 1887. The upper set of sidings was for general merchandise, with the lower set as a coal depot (marked 'out of use'); by the 1880s the Midland Railway was London's largest supplier of coal, and by 1900 was supplying more than 2,400,000 tons a year.

The sidings had a capacity of some 600 railway wagons, while at ground level were the distribution facilities – offices, stores, and even a large potato market – goods moving between the two by hydraulic power. Many hundreds of railway horses then delivered the goods around the capital.

The depot closed in 1973, the same year that the British Library was established by Act of Parliament. The site lay derelict until 1997, when the site of the southern half of the Somers Town yard was redeveloped as the Library; subsequently the northern half has become the Francis Crick Institute, a 'biomedical discovery institute researching the biology underlying human health'.

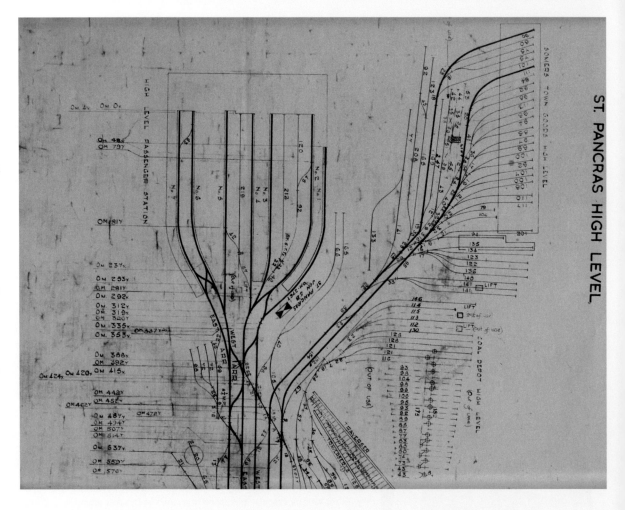

ST. PANCRAS HIGH LEVEL

SIGNAL PROFILE	ROUTE AVAILABILITY				
	ROUTE		ASPECT	FRONT ROUTE IND'R	BACK ROUTE IND'R
	DOWN HOME 1. PLATFORM 7 TO	DOWN GOODS	MAIN OR CALL-ON (RULE 44)	G	G
		WEST DEPARTURE	MAIN OR SHUNTING (RULE 47)	W	W
		EAST DEPARTURE		E	E
		UP FAST		U	U
		LOCO SIDINGS	SHUNTING (RULE 47)	SDG	SDG
	DOWN HOME 1. PLATFORM 6 TO	DOWN GOODS	MAIN OR CALL-ON (RULE 44)	G	G
		WEST DEPARTURE	MAIN OR SHUNTING (RULE 47)	W	W
		EAST DEPARTURE		E	E
		UP FAST		U	U
		LOCO SIDINGS	SHUNTING (RULE 47)	SDG	SDG
	DOWN HOME 1. PLATFORM 5 TO	DOWN GOODS	MAIN OR CALL-ON (RULE 44)	G	G
		WEST DEPARTURE	MAIN OR SHUNTING (RULE 47)	W	W
		EAST DEPARTURE		E	E
		UP FAST		U	U
	DOWN HOME 1. PLATFORM 4 TO	DOWN GOODS	MAIN OR CALL-ON (RULE 44)	G	G
		WEST DEPARTURE	MAIN OR SHUNTING (RULE 47)	W	W
		EAST DEPARTURE		E	E
	DOWN HOME 1. PLATFORM 3 TO	DOWN GOODS	MAIN OR CALL-ON (RULE 44)	G	G
		WEST DEPARTURE	MAIN OR SHUNTING (RULE 47)	W	W
		EAST DEPARTURE		E	E
	DOWN HOMES 1. PLATFORMS 1 & 2 TO	DOWN GOODS	MAIN OR CALL-ON (RULE 44)	G	G
		WEST DEPARTURE	MAIN OR SHUNTING (RULE 47)	W	W
		EAST DEPARTURE		E	E

ST PANCRAS On 8 May 1976 Class 45 No 45135 *3rd Carabinier* awaits departure from Platform 2. The new power signal box with its balcony is on the left. The signal is 'F' at the foot of the page from the new signalling 'Special Notice' booklet *(left)* – 'Down Homes 1' – signalling towards the West and East Departures and the Down Goods. The girders belong to bridge No 1 across Pancras Road, and the view beyond is dominated by those iconic gasholders.

The Class 45, originally No D99, is a little younger than the new signalling, having entered traffic in May 1961. Happily, it has outlived all the changes on its native Midland Main Line and survives in preservation. Withdrawn from service in March 1987, it spent its early preservation years at Peak Rail, moving to the East Lancashire Railway in June 1999. Mechanical problems led to it being taken out of service in 2007, and it is currently undergoing a full strip and rebuild by the Pioneer Diesel Locomotive Group.

To demonstrate the changes wrought at St Pancras, this is roughly the equivalent view today, at the country end of the original trainshed. Beyond the arch of the original is the 'transition roof' leading to what is described as the 'aluminium-clad louvre-blade and glass roof, giving north light', which covers the extended platforms for (straight ahead) East Midlands Trains, the current Midland Main Line operator, and on the right Eurostar services (beyond which are platforms serving Southeastern Railway domestic services). The roof covers all of what are now 13 platforms at the station. The escalators give access to the former undercroft, now 'The Arcade', featuring a variety of shops, cafes and the Eurostar departure lounge.

ST PANCRAS Prior to 1958 the station boasted two signal boxes, St Pancras Junction (opened in 1887 to control the station throat and access to the new Somers Town Goods Station), and St Pancras Passenger, a large double-size box with two back-to-back lever frames controlling entrance to and exit from the station's seven platforms. That changed on Sunday 6 October 1957 when these two boxes, together with Cambridge Street, closed and were replaced by a new power signal box, located at the country end of Platform 1 and brought into use the following day. As the BR Special Notice explained, 'The new signalling is designed to link up with the multi-aspect colour light signalling at Dock Junction and so provide continuous colour light signalling between St Pancras and Carlton Road Junction.' This extract from the accompanying signalling diagram shows the new arrangements. *Author's collection*

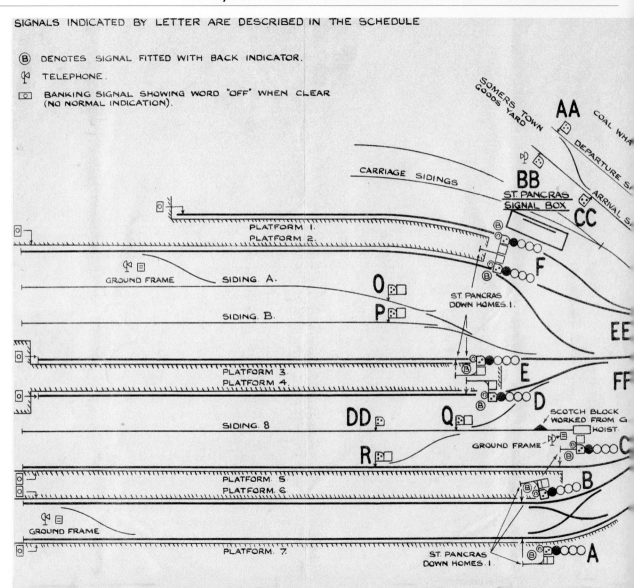

SIGNALS INDICATED BY LETTER ARE DESCRIBED IN THE SCHEDULE

Ⓑ DENOTES SIGNAL FITTED WITH BACK INDICATOR.

    TELEPHONE.

    BANKING SIGNAL SHOWING WORD "OFF" WHEN CLEAR (NO NORMAL INDICATION).

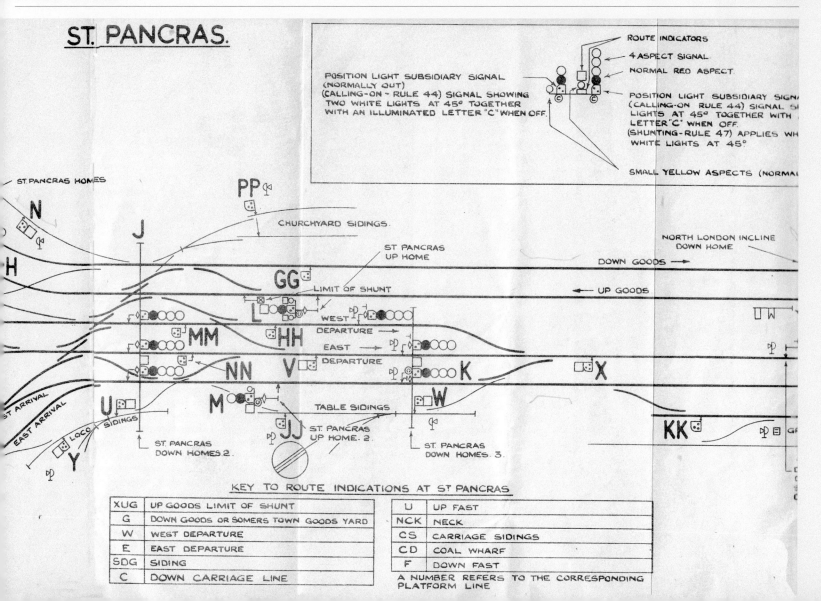

ST. PANCRAS.

ROUTE INDICATORS

4 ASPECT SIGNAL.

NORMAL RED ASPECT.

POSITION LIGHT SUBSIDIARY SIGNAL
(NORMALLY OUT)
(CALLING-ON - RULE 44) SIGNAL SHOWING
TWO WHITE LIGHTS AT 45° TOGETHER
WITH AN ILLUMINATED LETTER "C" WHEN OFF.

POSITION LIGHT SUBSIDIARY SIGNA
(CALLING-ON RULE 44) SIGNAL S
LIGHTS AT 45° TOGETHER WITH
LETTER "C" WHEN OFF.
(SHUNTING-RULE 47) APPLIES WH
WHITE LIGHTS AT 45°

SMALL YELLOW ASPECTS (NORMA

ST. PANCRAS HOMES

N

PP

CHURCHYARD SIDINGS.

ST PANCRAS
UP HOME

J

H

GG

NORTH LONDON INCLINE
DOWN HOME

DOWN GOODS →

LIMIT OF SHUNT

← UP GOODS

L

MM

HH

WEST

DEPARTURE →

EAST →

NN

V

DEPARTURE

K

X

M

U

TABLE SIDINGS

W

ST ARRIVAL

EAST ARRIVAL

LOCO   SIDINGS

Y

JJ

ST. PANCRAS
UP HOME. 2.

ST. PANCRAS
DOWN HOMES 2.

ST. PANCRAS
DOWN HOMES. 3.

KK

KEY TO ROUTE INDICATIONS AT ST PANCRAS

XUG	UP GOODS LIMIT OF SHUNT		U	UP FAST
G	DOWN GOODS OR SOMERS TOWN GOODS YARD		NCK	NECK
W	WEST DEPARTURE		CS	CARRIAGE SIDINGS
E	EAST DEPARTURE		CD	COAL WHARF
SDG	SIDING		F	DOWN FAST
C	DOWN CARRIAGE LINE			

A NUMBER REFERS TO THE CORRESPONDING
PLATFORM LINE

Above: **ST PANCRAS** On the other side of the old station, this was the view from Platform 7, also on 8 May 1976. The signals are, on the right, 'A' in the page from the 1958 booklet, and on the left 'B'. In the distance, beyond the bridge, can be seen the concrete roof of the coal chutes on Pancras Road beside Churchyard Sidings. Of most interest, however, are the white railings at the end of Platforms 5/6; these protected a wagon hoist giving access to the undercroft below.

Above right: **ST PANCRAS** Wagons full of beer barrels from Bass and various other brewers were pulled into the station, then reversed onto the hydraulic lift, which was big enough to accommodate a wagon and the horse pulling it. At ground level, beneath the platforms, two railway lines ran the length of the stores, with three wagon turntables allowing them to be manoeuvred throughout. As is well-known, the 688 (or, according to another

source, 720) cast-iron pillars in the undercroft supporting the station deck were spaced 14ft 8in apart, as in the beer warehouses at Burton-upon-Trent, which was a multiple of the diameter of a beer barrel, thereby maximising the storage space. As the station's designer and engineer, William Barlow, said, 'The length of a beer barrel became the unit of measure upon which all the arrangements of this floor were based.' This specially created cellar was so large that at one time three dedicated trains of beer arrived daily. The hydraulic hoist had its own ground frame, with a scotch block to prevent wagons rolling into the void when the hoist was at the lower level. Over time, other businesses such as beer bottlers and brewers' agents used the undercroft, but its use gradually declined and it closed to beer traffic on 1 July 1963, after which the space was let to third parties and further subdivided; the hoist was taken out of use six months later.

The flat-roofed building beside the hoist sits on the site of the former large St Pancras Passenger signal box, displaced by the new one on the left in 1958.

Left: **ST PANCRAS** Immediately beyond the Pancras Road bridge on the right, above Goods Way, were the gasholders of the former Imperial Gas Light & Coke Co, which had been established beside the Regent's Canal in 1822. The gasholders were erected in the 1850s; some were later Grade II listed, and remained in use until 2000. As part of the regeneration of the St Pancras/King's Cross area, gasholder No 8, together with the triplet set of Nos 10, 11 and 12, were dismantled and shipped piece by piece to Yorkshire, where they were restored before returning to be rebuilt at their new home a little further north overlooking St Pancras lock near where the railway crosses the canal. The triplet set contains circular apartment blocks, while No 8, the largest, which once held 1.1 million cubic feet of gas, is a public open space known as Gasholder Park.

Also seen here alongside the old loco sidings is the very ornate Gothic water tower, containing a large cast-iron tank with a capacity of almost 14,000 gallons to supply water to steam locos. Because of its location it was threatened with demolition, so with help from English Heritage, lottery funding and other parties, it was carefully removed in 2001 to a new site where the railway crosses Camley Street.

The second picture is more or less the same view, looking north at ground level. The Pancras Road bridge is now completely under the new extended station, at the traffic lights seen here. The new Camley Street is straight ahead, where the retaining wall once was, with Goods Way off to the right before the trees that line Camley Street Natural Park. This local nature reserve opened in 1985, and has since benefitted from the recent redevelopment of the area. In the distance can be seen the water tower in its new location.

Right: It was decided that dismantling and rebuilding the water tower was not practicable, so it was separated into sections, each weighing some 125 and 135 tons, and moved about 700 metres by road to its new home overlooking the St Pancras Yacht Basin, where it is leased to British Waterways Board and used by St Pancras Cruising Club. After repairs and refurbishment it was opened to the public in 2005.

ST PANCRAS Journey's end … or beginning. On 21 February 1976 the archway beneath the Hotel leads to the former arrival-side cab road, which occupied the wide space between Platforms 5 and 6; originally the cabs arrived by means of a ramp from Pancras Road at the end of the platform and exited through this arch and down the slope to Euston Road. This broad platform was later used for loading mail and newspapers. Note the sooty blackness of the brickwork and a general feeling of neglect.

　　Today the brickwork and polished columns sparkle like new following the spectacular restoration of the building. Beyond the arch the view is now of the glass screens surrounding the Eurostar platforms. Note the empty niches, which were designed to contain statues; I believe that these were omitted from the original design as a cost-saving measure, the building having severely overrun its budget.

ST PANCRAS At the eastern end of the hotel on the corner of Pancras Road is this 270-foot-tall spire-capped clock tower. The clock was supplied by John Walker of Cornhill in 1872, and it worked on for almost a century before old age caught up with it and it stopped in 1967. Once again, the architectural glory is lost beneath a patina of London soot.

ST PANCRAS The eminent Gothic Revival architect Sir George Gilbert Scott was awarded the contract to design the Midland Grand Hotel, the building that would fill the southern end of Barlow's trainshed and provide the Midland Railway's magnificent and prestigious 'calling card' on Euston Road, in my opinion the finest Gothic building in London, if not the country. (Scott himself wrote, 'It is often spoken of to me as the finest building in London; my own belief is that it is possibly *too good* for its purpose…')

The station had been in use for several years before the hotel was finally completed in 1876, having cost almost half a million pounds. With lifts ('ascending chambers'), concrete floors, revolving doors and a fireproof floor construction, it was one of the most modern and best appointed hotels in the capital.

The hotel prospered until after the First World War, when decline set in, and it was considered old-fashioned (especially its lack of en-suite bathrooms) and too expensive to run. It closed in April 1935 and became 'St Pancras Chambers', used as railway offices, in particular as the headquarters of, appropriately, British Transport Hotels. It gained Grade I listing in the 1960s, following an unsuccessful plan to demolish it, but in the 1980s the building failed its fire certificate and was closed down, to remain empty for many years.

In the mid-1990s £10 million was spent by BR and English Heritage on restoring the exterior and making the building structurally sound and weatherproof. The interior had been unsympathetically converted into drab office accommodation, but happily many of the original features survived. Then, with the advent of the station's new 'International' role, in 2004 planning permission was granted for its redevelopment into a new hotel. Today's St Pancras Renaissance Hotel, part of the Marriott group, contains 244 bedrooms, two restaurants, two bars, a health and leisure centre, a ballroom, and 20 meeting and function rooms. The upper floors were redeveloped as 68 apartments by the Manhattan Loft Corporation. The new hotel's formal Grand Opening was on 5 May 2011 – exactly 138 years after its original opening in 1873. The clock is presumably working again, as it was telling the correct time when I took the present-day photograph!

'Renaissance' is an appropriate name for the hotel as, although no longer in railway ownership, it symbolises the remarkable rebirth of the Midland Railway's extension to London, from the tired, unloved line I photographed in the late 1970s to the shiny new electric railway of today.

A room key from the original hotel. *Author's collection*